TABLE OF CONTENTS

He Restores My Soul	1
Not Destroyed	4
Recharge	8
We Are Overcomers	12
You Have What It Takes	15
Contending For The Faith	18
It's Time To Arise	21
Life In Christ	24
No Worries	27
New Day…New Season	30
Praise Break….	33
Rest	37
God Is With Us	40
God Morning	43
A Blessing In Disguise	46
The Past Is The Past	50
Don't Move	53
Break-Through	57

TABLE OF CONTENTS

The "Be" Attitudes	60
Wisdom Speaks	64
Jesus is M.I.A.	67
Pray Through It	70
No Limits	73
I Can See Clearly Now	76
Be Faithful	79
Be Still and Know	82
Fresh Oil, Fresh Fire	85
Growth Mindset	88
Reset	91
Encourage Yourself Again	94
Words of Life & Hope	97
ABOUT THE AUTHOR	130

ENCOURAGE YOURSELF IN THE LORD V2.

META J. TOWNSAND

Encourage Yourself In The Lord
Vol. 2

Copyright © 2021 by Meta J. Townsand

All rights reserved. No portion of this book may be reproduced, stored in a retrieval system, or transmitted in any form or by any means – electronic, mechanical, photocopy, recording, scanning, or other – except for brief quotations in critical reviews or articles, without prior written permission of the publisher.

Published in Grand Rapids, Michigan by Meta J. Towsand.

Unless otherwise noted, scripture quotations in this book are from The Holy Bible, New International Version®, NIV®, Copyright © 1973, 1978, 1984, 2011 by Biblical, Inc.™. Published by Zondervan. www.zondervan.com

ISBN: 978-0-9963256-6-0

Book cover design by Freda Tolbert

Book formatting by Oracle Publishing, a subsidiary of Oracle Media Group, LLC.

Image provided by Adobe Stock file # 306487786

Printed in the United States of America.

DEDICATION

I am so grateful to God, for His source of strength along this journey called life. We often say, "if it had not been for the Lord on my side, where would I be...?" Truly, I am thankful for God's unfailing hand.

Therefore, I dedicate these writings to those who get discouraged, frustrated, overwhelmed sometimes with the cares of this life; to those who know that retreating isn't an option; to those who need a daily reminder and "pick me up"; to those who are contemplating giving up.... Don't you dare!!

When the way gets tough and almost unbearable, we learn to encourage ourselves in the Lord, just as David did.

HE RESTORES MY SOUL

The Lord is my shepherd, I shall not want. He makes me to lie down in green pastures, he leads me beside the quiet waters, He restores my soul.

Psalm 23:1-3

The role of a "good" shepherd in herding sheep is to provide nourishment, covering, protection, grooming, leadership and guidance. When sheep go astray, it is the role of the shepherd to go find the sheep and restore them to a place of safety. It is also believed that sheep are really dumb animals and they often will find themselves in precarious situations that the shepherd will have to come and rescue them.

Sometimes in life we stray from our purpose; we follow after things and people; we lose focus; we get burned out because of the demands that others or ourselves have placed on us; we get frustrated and throw in the towel; we lose our way and get tired; we get discouraged and want to give up. But the word says that He Restores Us.

See, **restore means to bring back**. Some of us need to come back from being destroyed and out for the count. **Restore means to reinstate**. Some of us have lost our flavor, our vitality, our position and after we come back from the end of ourselves, we need to get back into the right state. **Restore means to return.** After we have tried and done things our own way, we need to return to The Way. Can I tell you that Jesus Only, can fill the voids and emptiness you may feel in your life! After you have come to the end, only He can restore you to life.

There is a hiding place, a rock that we run to, when the way gets hard to find. Psalm 23, is one of my favorite scriptures, the first scripture I ever memorized, the scripture I mostly recite at the dinner table before we eat and the scripture that has come to be so meaningful to me in life. It reminds us that the Lord is our true shepherd. Therefore, our wanting is in Him. Our resting is in Him. Our comfort is in Him. Our peace is in Him. Our being is in Him. Our joy is in Him. Our restoration is in Him. Our life is in him and He will take care of us in whatever state that we may find ourselves in. I've learned and continue to learn that ANYTHING outside of Him is temporary.

So, if you're feeling drained and spent, allow the Father to restore your soul....

NOT DESTROYED

Hard pressed on every side, but not crushed; perplexed, but not in despair; persecuted, but not abandoned; struck down, but not destroyed.

2 Corinthians 4:8-9

Even though you may be feeling frustration, feeling defeated, facing a storm, involved in an insurmountable dilemma, not liking where you are, in a fiery furnace or looking down the throat of a roaring lion, can I just say that you are NOT destroyed. We know that the enemy comes to kill, steal and destroy, BUT GOD, comes in to interject, intervene, and to change our perspective on the matter because He gives us life. We have life in the fact that God's abundance of grace, love, joy, mercy and strength causes us to triumph over the situation. We may feel like we won't make it, BUT GOD, wakes us up the next morning to try again, to live again, to pursue again under His new grace and mercy in our lives.

We have an advocate, Jesus, who is praying for us because satan is desiring to sift us as wheat. In studying the process of sifting, there is a violent procedure of threshing and beating as the grain needs to separate from the stalk. If you can get this picture, the enemy is asking to violently separate us, snatch us, pull us from the love of God, the grace of God's goodness, the Word of God that's in our heart and mind, to actually wear out the fabric of our faith. (Some of you may feel like he's doing just that). However, just as you are reading this chapter now, I declare in your spirit that God is ever present and through this, you are strong in His strength.

According to Webster's dictionary, destroyed means you are demolished, ruined, erased, annihilated, wiped out, obliterated, eradicated, finished or utterly defeated. David says in Psalms 27: 13 that he would have fainted unless he had seen the goodness of the Lord. Can't we all really testify to that? If God hadn't stepped in, (omg), I would have lost my mind, given up, thrown in the towel, walked away, BUT there was a BUT GOD at the other end, meeting me in my dilemma.

One of my favorite shows is Property Brothers on the HGTV Channel. I read an article in the US Magazine that told their story of bankruptcy, one of them a failed marriage and one of them suffering from depression. Nevertheless, the article shared how they were able to bounce back from what could have made the average person give up and walk away. They took advantage of a second chance and are multimillionaires with various business deals that are successful.

How much more does God allow and give us second chances to get up again, to live again, or to try again. Our setbacks and failures should be and can be stepping stones to success, if we just take the time to think differently about where we are and where we need to go. The lessons we learn along the way are meant to help us endure hardship like a "G" (good soldier) to be of good cheer, while we wait on God; to stand firm while we suffer (a little while) because "this" doesn't come to destroy us, but to refine us; to improve us, purify us, polish us, and to make us. We are resilient to be better and not bitter. There is a double portion promised to us, if we stay the course.

In the first 10 years of our marriage, Larry and I were struggling and tripping (LOL), that resulted in us separating for about 9 months. Even though I can laugh now, it wasn't funny back then because I was mad at what the enemy was trying to do. In learning hard lessons, self-examination, humbling myself, praying and standing, there was an answer to prayer that could have easily turned into a bitter divorce.

Can I tell you that out of the situation of reconciliation, I received a double portion of cookware, dishes, household items that I was planning on purchasing in the future. Now, I don't recommend we get a double portion in this manner (lol), however, God turned this situation around for the good and I received a double portion out of the deal. The point being is that God can bless us in immeasurable ways and dimensions, if we can just be steady and stay the course. I promise you, there is a blessing at the end of this, ask Job!!

RECHARGE

He led me back and forth among them, and I saw a great many bones on the floor of the valley, bones that were very dry. He asked me, "Son of man, can these bones live?"

Ezekiel 37:2-3

Reboot, Restore, Revive, Renew, Regain, Reset, Replenish, Recover = RECHARGE

We all have cell phones, right? The only way that our phones work is by it being charged over and over and over again. In order for the phone to receive the charge needed for usage, it has to get plugged into a power source for a period of time until it is full. When we find that the phone is not "holding a charge", we purchase a new battery or better yet upgrade to another phone with more capabilities and more power.

In our lives we face hardships, storms, setbacks, trials, trouble, demands of life and whatever else that will drain our energy, strength and life. If we aren't careful, we may find ourselves depleted physically, mentally and spiritually. Now, we can easily get some sleep, go on vacation or close our door to meet our physical and mental needs, but what do we do to recharge our spiritual needs.

In this day and hour, we are facing and encountering major concerns in the nation, families, young people, finances, societal systems, communities and churches that are leaving God's people tired and worn. They are on the front line in prayer and not receiving the daily dosage of bread and water (or they're not in prayer and depending on their own strength...let's just call it out). Even though we may feel hard pressed, this is definitely the time to stay connected and be encouraged with the Giver of life.

God asks the prophet Ezekiel an interesting question, "Can these bones live?" This indicates to me that the bones he's referring to have been in the valley a long time and now they have become dry, lifeless and unproductive. Sometimes, we are in our valley seasons a long time without spiritual bread and water resulting in dry, brittle, fireless praise and worship. We have become numb to the things around us and we find ourselves just going through the motions. BUT, Honey, the dry bones in you can live again. The purpose in your life can live again. The dreams that you have can live again. After 20 years, my books are coming to life...come on here, somebody. I declare and decree over your life that YOU will live in spite of the valley!

God is not through with you yet, so why are you through with you? God still has purpose and every obstacle you may have encountered to get you to this place doesn't have to remain, when God is allowed to breath afresh and new in your life. When God breathes, dreams come alive (like I'm continuing to write this book in this season), energy emerges, opportunities and open doors become available, invitations to tables of influence are extended, divine connections present itself. And before you know it, God has enlarged your territory.

Seasonal valleys will come, but don't park there too long that you miss the moments for mountainous experiences. One thing for sure is that valleys (troubles) don't last all ways (unless you want it to).

WE ARE OVERCOMERS

And they overcame him because of the blood and the word of their testimony.

Revelation 12:11

Through these pages, can I tell you that no matter what you are going through and/or are facing, You can overcome. I know it may be easy for me to say because I'm not in your shoes. However, I've had "shoes" to wear and had to learn to overcome some things if I planned on living the God-life.

According to Webster's dictionary, to Overcome means to succeed in dealing with a problem, situation or difficulty. In other words, to get the better of, prevail over, get control of, conquer or defeat, to solve, to get a grip on (get these adjectives) to get over, to lick, to beat, to triumph.

God has given us strategies to help us overcome in this life. We know we have His Word; we know we have His Promises; we know we have the work of the cross and the Blood, but what is the word from your testimony. What words of life do you speak over yourself, about your situation or about the God that you believe and serve? What is coming out of your mouth when you are faced with other's opinions of you, when a disappointment or frustration comes, when you make a mistake? We are surrounded with a wealth of living witnesses that have been where we are and live to tell the story. The Word tells us that we can declare and decree and watch things happen. The Word tells us to speak life and not death. I'm a big believer that if God did it for someone else (them), He can do it for me (us).

Life will give us some setbacks from time to time, but we learn the lessons of not getting bitter and the lessons of how to move on. Some may be easier than others, but that's where you dig in and be intentional to overcome all the "shots" that will try and impact you in a negative manner. We must learn to overcome our past to be able to live in our present that will prepare us for our future. God cannot get us to our future, if we don't learn to overcome the temporary obstacles.

You can do this and live.

YOU HAVE WHAT IT TAKES

I felt I had to write and urge you to contend for the faith that was once for all entrusted to the saints.

Jude 3

Faith grows as a result of the Word in us and the relationship and experiences (trials, mistakes, cares of life) we have with Christ. Let's consider the experiences David had with the Lord when it came to fighting the lion, that he conquered, the bear that he conquered, and ultimately goliath that he conquered. Each experience gave him more and more confidence in what God called him to be and to do.

It's our faith in God that sustains us, helps us and strengthens us in times and when times come knocking at our doors. Remember Jesus told Peter that he was praying that his faith would not fail because he knew what Peter would have to face and he didn't want him to fail. And I get it, standing, believing, trusting faith may not always be easy, but, it sure can't be passive. Sometimes, we just have to fight or contend for the faith, sometimes in varying degrees, but at least fight.

Contending Faith:
- Fights against the negativity, and shuts out the distractions (the noise that drown out our own thoughts at times)

- Keeps affirming what you know to be true
- Strives to achieve your assignment
- Deals with difficult situations and sometimes people
- Contends with the enemy of your past, future and your mind

A scripture that blesses my heart every time I read it, is found in 2 Peter 1:3. It says, His divine power has given us everything we need for life and godliness....

Faith is our godliness to have and to hold from this day forward.

CONTENDING FOR THE FAITH

And without faith it is impossible to please God because anyone that comes to Him must believe that He exists and that He rewards those that diligently seek Him.

Hebrews 11:6

How do you contend for the faith and fight against distractions, negativity and opposition to your assignments? Let's take our cues from Nehemiah.

Pray: 1: 1-11

Seek wisdom: 2: 4

Ask for help: 4:4-5, 9

Encounter strength: 6: 9

Strategize 4:13-21: Nehemiah had to watch and pray, build and pray, get instruction and build, get the weapons of warfare and build and work smarter, not harder (in other words, know when and how to work the assignment given to you).

Discernment 6:1-9: Nehemiah knew what his enemies were up to. He was not carried away by flattery or enticed by what appeared to be good and wasn't. The

Bible says he couldn't be intimated to commit a sin by doing contrary to what God had given him to do (that's good right there). The Bible tells us that the enemy cannot outwit us, if we're not ignorant of his devices (1 Corinthians 2:11)

Speak to the mountain 4:14-15 and 6:8-9. You cannot lose your voice in times of trouble. Nehemiah knew to encourage those that were with and around him to complete the tasks at hand. He knew to put words in the atmosphere that would bring about life and change.

Continue the work 6:15-16. Nehemiah didn't allow what was said or what was tried to diminish his faith in what he was assigned to do. We put our hands to the plow and we move forward knowing that God is the author and finisher of our faith.

ITS TIME TO ARISE

Arise and shine, for the light has come, and the glory of the Lord has risen upon you.

Isaiah 60:1

We used to sing a song in the choir (Yes, in the days of the choir) "Zion is calling you to a higher place of praise. To stand on the mountain and to magnify His name. To tell all the people of every nation that He reigns. Zion is calling you to a higher place of praise". (Stephen Hurd)

I believe that God is calling us out of complacency and procrastination to become a voice of influence. During one of our hosted "Intercessors Arise" gatherings, Minister Terrell Wheat led the participants in an activity asking them to estimate the number of people or groups that they're affiliated with. The purpose of this exercise was to show the power of influence, positive or negative. In our group we realized that we had the potential of touching or influencing over a billion people. Think about this. How much information do we receive, and in turn share that information with someone, and in turn they share that information with someone else? That's powerful!

When we live in a world and seasons of uncertainty, confusion and fears, God is still calling us to arise. Let His light shine that he has given us and not be silent, but to have an answer for those that are seeking the truth. He calls us to influence systems and people in places where we are and have been "strategically" placed.

We are called to be light in the darkness, but how many times have men and women of God been sucked up or got caught up in this worldly system of compromise, backdoor dealings and deceit. So, if we think we have nothing to offer, well think again, because we do. No matter our age, no matter what others think or what we think about ourselves, every day God gives us, is an opportunity to yield to God what He has given you. From time to time, I experience "backlash" for being a voice for students and families. However, the "backlash" cannot discourage me from doing what God has called me to do in arising and speaking up, supporting and helping those that God has put in my path. We are His workmanship in the earth to do of His good pleasure (Ephesians 2:10).

Arise, take your place because you belong.

LIFE IN CHRIST

For in Him we live and move and have our being. As some of your own poets have said, We are His offspring.

Acts 17:28

Our life cannot and is not defined by trouble, circumstances or the cares of life that we experience. It is the job of the enemy to remind us, condemn us, shame us in our past life (Before Christ) and in this life (In Christ). But scripture interrupts our thinking to remind and tell us that there is No condemnation to those that are in Christ Jesus. There is no disapproval, criticism, denunciation or punishment in Him. Through Christ Spirit of love, we are free to live life.

Naturally speaking, we find our life, our identity, our worth, our value from our families. However, if our families struggled to give us the identity and life we needed to function in society, we got "jacked up"...lets just call it out. BUT, BUT, BUT, BUT, BUT God knows and cares for those that belong to Him. He gives new life. If you can go down memory lane, you can say that God had HIS hand on you. When other people got caught, you didn't. When other people were exposed, you weren't. When other people found it hard, you didn't. When other people died, you were spared....come on!! The Bible tells us that the goodness of the Lord, brings us to a place of repentance. That repentance brings us to a place to make an exchange of life (old) for a life in Him (new).

One of my favorite scriptures is from 2 Corinthians 5:17 that says, we are new creations in Christ, Old things have passed away and behold, all things become new. What a comfort that is to know. Anything, that we have ever done is under the blood and we have been redeemed to live a different kind of life. We have become "sons" of the Father, therefore, aligning our identity to Him. Because we have life in Him, we have access to the throne room of Grace, Help, Benefits, Protection, Mediation and Success.

Choose the God kind of life. It can be yours for the asking.

(At this time, if you are reading this chapter and you are in a backslidden state, or in need of the Father, please pray with me: "Dear Jesus, please forgive me of my sins and my unrighteousness. I forgive others that have sinned against me, as I forgive others. I believe you are the Son of God and that you died for me. I receive the life that you have ordained for my life by faith, and I ask you to fill me with your Spirit. I ask you to come into my heart. Give me help, wisdom and guidance to live in Jesus Name.")

NO WORRIES

Be anxious for nothing, but in everything by prayer and petition with thanksgiving, present your request to God.

Philippians 4:7

One of the famous saying from the movie Lion King is "hakuna matata" which means, "No Worries". The Bible also confirms that belief in Matthew 6. It says not to worry about your life. He takes care of the birds and lilies in the field, therefore He can take care of you, as you have more value. Besides, whose worry is adding any value, productivity and fruitfulness to their life?

Unexpected things happen in life all the time that will make us concerned and worried about what may come next, but trusting, holding on, and relying on a God who gives us life and joy will not fail. If He has taken care of us in the past, then why would He not take care of us now?

As I am a parent and know the concerns I have about my children, I turn to prayer (and sometimes still worry). Sometimes, I wonder if and how my parents worried over me, especially when I found myself in many a situation that I was ashamed of and knew I wasn't raised as such and to this day would not dare tell them. In my reflection of the past, I know it had to be their prayers that God honored that kept me along the way (and to this day). In turn, as my children tell me snippets of their experiences and knowing they weren't raised in such a way, I remember those times that they were with friends or at a party or something I asked them not to do and they did anyway and that the Lord kept them. As parents we do worry about our children, but a promise from God says, what we commit to Him, He will keep.

For some of you that struggle to overcome anxiety and worry, you have to be intentional to not have your thoughts run away with ideas and thoughts that will never happen. The remedy is to pray and petition with thanksgiving your needs to Him. Then God promises to give us peace! We need to protect that peace and not allow any foreign thoughts to invade our thinking that doesn't align with His Word or His promises over our life. The comfort is that no matter where we are in life, God got us!

NEW DAY...NEW SEASON

SEE, I am doing a new thing, will you not perceive it?

Isaiah 43:19

In order for the new to come, change has to come. Oftentimes, we don't equate change with the birthing of the new because we become familiar with what we have. If we unpack that concept, God tells us that He is doing a new thing in our lives and in the earth. Doing, is a word of action for the new that's happening. However, in order for the new to take root, there has to be change. You cannot have a Spring without the change from Fall and you cannot have Fall without the change from Summer. Therefore, you cannot have the new in your life without the ending of the old.

One thing for sure, change is not popular, but change is inevitable. It will come whether you're ready for it or not. We can become extinct or irrelevant if we refuse to embrace the new that God has for us. We often talk about going from "glory to glory." Well that comes through change. New seasons of productivity come through change. Improvements come into our lives when we change. Nothing can become something unless we change. Change what? Change our perspective? Change our mind? Change our behavior? Change our attitude? Change our company? WOW!

The caterpillar would not become a beautiful butterfly unless it went through the process of metamorphosis. If you want new seasons in your life:

1. **Obey instructions**: learn to do what needs to be done.

2. **Trust God in the Process:** learn to not lean to your own understanding, but acknowledge Him and He will direct your path.

3. **Sacrifice:** we cannot sacrifice to God that which will not cost us something.

Our "See" is often times attached to the "Seek" that we have been asking about. Of course, we don't like the Covid 19 Pandemic, but I believe that it could be in "the seek" that change happens in the earth. If we can see that through this, in this, and in spite of this, God is doing something new in the earth that will yield forth His coming, His truth, His salvation, His Kingdom, His glory, His power to be revealed. It's ugly and messy, but we "See" the good that will be and has been produced.

PRAISE BREAK

The weapons of our warfare are not carnal but mighty through the pulling down of strongholds.

2 Corinthians 10:5

So, let's praise!

I will bless the Lord at all times, His Praise shall continually be in my mouth. My soul will boast in the Lord; let the afflicted hear and rejoice. Come magnify the Lord with me; let us exalt his name together.

Psalm 34: 1-3

Bless the Lord, O my soul; all my inmost being, praise his holy name. Praise the Lord, O my soul and forget not all his benefits- who forgives all your sins and heals all your diseases, who redeems your life from the pit and crowns you with love and compassion who satisfies your desires with good things so that your youth is renewed like the eagle's.

Psalm 103: 1-5

Clap your hands all you nations; shout to God with cries of joy. How awesome is the Lord Most High, the great King over all the earth!

Psalm 47: 1-2

I will praise you, O Lord, with all my heart; I will tell if all your wonders. I will be glad and rejoice in you; I will sing praise to your name, O Most High.

Psalm 9:1-2

Praise be to the Lord, to God our Savior, who daily bears our burdens. Our God is a God who saves; from the Sovereign Lord comes escape from death

Psalm 68:19-20

Come, let us sing for joy to the Lord; let us shout aloud to the Rock of our salvation. Let us come before him with thanksgiving and extol him with music and song. For the Lord is the great God, the great King above all gods.

Psalm 95: 1-3

Shout to the Lord, all the earth. Worship the Lord with gladness, come before his presence with singing. Know that the Lord is God. It is He who made us, and we are his; we are his people, the sheep of his pasture. Enter into his gates with thanksgiving and his courts with praise; give thanks to him and bless his name. For the Lord is good and his mercy endures forever; his faithfulness continues through all generations.

Psalm 100

Let everything that has breath, praise the Lord, Praise the Lord!

Psalm 150: 6

REST

He makes me lie down in green pastures, he leads me beside quiet waters.

Psalm 23: 2

      One of the hardest things for Americans to do or people who consider themselves movers and shakers, is to rest. Even though or all though time waits for no one (Geoffrey Chaucer), we still have to be about our Father's business. However, we recognize that procrastination is the enemy of productivity. Nevertheless, there are times that it is required that we slow down, take the time and rest. Rest, not only our bodies, but our minds. Rest, to evaluate where we've been, where we are and where we need to go. Rest and get refueled for the journey. Rest and examine our priorities. Rest and exhale.

      During this national pandemic of the coronavirus, we are surely in a place of rest, physically, mentally and spiritually. Physically, because we really can't go anywhere. We have been forced to slow our lives down. (Me, included, I'm able to get the much needed "sleep" that I've been missing). Mentally, because you can stop to rationally think through the issues and cares of life and not always be "reactionary." And spiritually, because there is a rest in God that takes us away from the hustle, bustle and busyness of the day. There's a "rest" in God that allows all of our concerns, cares and anxieties to dissipate.

God invites us to a place of resting in Him, just sitting with Him before we start our day, sometimes, in the middle of the day and as we come to the end of our day. As much as we have our calendars filled, can I tell you, that you are not the energizer bunny...lol (and neither do you have to be). I am always appreciative of the times that I can really enjoy my coffee talks with the Lord. It allows me time to read the Word and commune with the Father, just to rest and enjoy in and with Him. The "spirit of Martha" in me becomes the "spirit of Mary" that draws me to take a seat at the feet of Jesus.

Come unto me all you who are laboring and I will give you rest....Invitation by Jesus!!

GOD IS WITH US

He said, Look! I see four men walking around in the fire, unbound and unharmed, and the fourth looks like a son of the gods.

Daniel 3:25

    In the seasons of our lives that bring uncertainties, misfortunes, or loss, we have to know, that we don't go through the hard seasons of life alone. We may feel alone, but we're not alone. We may feel like we're in the trenches by ourselves, but we're not alone. We may feel like nobody cares, but we're not alone. We may feel like we're so overwhelmed and not going to make it, but **we are not alone.**

    Our confidence has to be in the Lord of our salvation. Our hope and trust has to be in the creator of all. If you really think about it, you may have been in this place before, but in a different time, with different characters or different scenario, but you made it. You got through it. Your strength and help came from the Lord, bottom line. And if truth be told, you aren't wearing the clothes or residue of what you've been through. And if truth be told, no one would know you've been through or in a battle unless you testify and show your battle scars.

The Bible says that when the 3 Hebrews boys were thrown in the fiery furnace, they had such confidence in God to see them through. The God they served was well able to save them; watch this, and even if he didn't, they were not going to bow. Daniel 3: 26b testifies that when Shadrach, Meshach and Abednego came out of the fire, they (government officials) saw that the fire had not harmed their bodies, not a hair on their heads singed; their robes were not scorched and there was no smell of fire on them.

Elder and I went through a season where we had to file bankruptcy. It was a hard decision made after reviewing our financial records in addition to receiving misinformation about what our payment plan would be. As a result, it caused Larry, I believe, to retire before the time. It caused a breach in confidentiality with a dear friend. In reality, there wasn't a reduced payment plan (wah, wah). We had to pay full price (our fiery furnace). Nevertheless, can I tell you that God was with us. We were still blessed. Bills still got paid, we still had food on our table. It taught us discipline, and when things got bad or broke down GOD always had a ram in the bush!! My God, He got us through our fiery furnace, and we didn't smell like what we had been through.

WOW, that is amazing! As it was for them and for us, it can be so for you. Our comfort in life is that no matter what, no matter what, NO MATTER WHAT, God got us!

GOD MORNING

I will bless the Lord at all times; his praise shall continually be on my lips.

Psalm 34:1

My brother, Matthew's (1961-2019) morning greeting was "God Morning." He didn't believe in a good morning, but a God morning that led to an inspired day. He would tell you in a minute that God woke us up in the morning, therefore make it a God day, so we have to give Him praise.

Watching Deacon Matthew Brinkley exhort the Lord and encourage the Sunday congregation to praise the Lord was always a "godly treat." God never ceases to amaze me at the way He moves in the lives of people. So, witnessing my dear brother and having our family together for Sunday worship was always a blessing.

Matt took the days in stride, that no matter what came his way, he always reached back to give God the credit. He was a big spender, a big dreamer, a big giver with a big heart that served in various capacities. He knew that the life God gave him was not his own, so he loved and accepted whatever God allowed and did. His email and one of his motto scriptures is from Matthew 22: 37-39, Love the Lord your God with all your heart and with all your soul and with all your mind. This is the first and greatest commandment. And the second is like it: Love your neighbor as yourself.

Matthew transitioned this life after doing what he does so well, testifying to the goodness of the Lord to our Monday's Prayer Call Group. He shared his faith and died in the Faith, being among the cloud of witnesses that believed even though he didn't get the opportunity to see that which he believed. He lived as if he had it already because it was a God Day to him.

So, our good mornings are not just good, but God mornings because He makes them good.

(Miss you a bunch Matt)

A BLESSING IN DISGUISE

For this momentary light affliction is producing for us and eternal weight of glory far beyond all comparison.

2 Corinthians 4:17

No one sees the loss of a job as a blessing because that can imply lost wages. No one sees the loss of a spouse as a blessing because that can imply loneliness. No one sees the loss of an important relationship as a blessing because that can imply a conflict. No one sees the loss of health as a blessing because that can imply death. No one sees the loss of a marital union as a blessing because that can imply failure. No one sees the loss of material possessions (house or car) that sustain us in life as a blessing because that can imply poverty. No one sees the loss of freedom (as we know it in America today) as a blessing because it can imply our insecurities.

Well Beloved, I believe that God has temporarily interrupted our lives to get our attention. Every day he sounds the alarms, speaks to us in nature, ministers to us through various men and women of God, guides us in His Word, and shows us great and mighty things. Yet, we go about our lives wanting what we know to be as normal.

You may not want to read or believe this, but loss can actually be a good thing, if and when we get past the pain of it all - including how it looks and feels. If we can be honest, facing loss allows us a space for healthy reflection and evaluation. That when we come through it, we are better and wiser. We are wiser in how we treat others or how others should treat us. We are wiser in how we spend our money. We are wiser in taking care of our resources. We are wiser in our responses to people, places and things. We are wiser in how we take care of our bodies. We are wiser in spending our time with the Lord.

If you think of a 4-way traffic signal, no one direction can continue to pass through the intersection without slowing down (yellow light) and eventually stopping (red light). In our lives, we have pauses, subtle changes or warning signs (yellow lights) to slow down BEFORE the red lights in life make us STOP and take note. This is a funny reflective thought, then we act like we didn't see it coming (me included....).

A different perspective is taking the time not to freak out, but examine how we got here, and what to do next. We can never be without the guidance of God in prayer, confession, repentance and asking. The blessing in the loss is the fact that God loves us enough for us to get it right. He loves us enough to stop us from self-destruction. He loves us enough to release us from toxic people and things. He loves us enough to help us start over. He loves us enough to give us time to be healed and whole. He loves us enough to lead us in returning to our first love, which is Him.

So, we all have been touched by this pandemic in some form or fashion. We all have, are experiencing the shut-downs and stay at home orders by the states and approved by God. Let's look at this to our gain as we turn our heart, mind, body and soul, to the God of our salvation. This has been a blessing in disguise for us to slow down and take note, the Lord is at hand.

THE PAST IS THE PAST

But one thing I do: forgetting what is behind and straining toward what is ahead, I press.

Philippians 3:13-14a

Memories can sometimes be unsettling and painful. On the other hand, they can be used for your benefit in empowering you for your future. Pain, (we all have them) whether by you or someone else can be the launching pad towards your purpose in the earth, IF, you don't stay in a place of being defeated.

A stronger life of prayer was birthed out of my experiences of pain and disappointments. Having a heart for intercession was birthed out of knowing what God did for me and what HE can do for others. Having a heart to encourage married women was birthed out of my own marital problems. Having a heart for souls was birthed out of hearing and seeing the plight of people as they navigate life. A hunger for righteousness and the things of God was birthed out of a life of being separated from God and wanting Him because of the Word, His love and great mercies towards me. Therefore, in turn I had a desire to be a blessing to All (Believers and Non-believers) in sharing the good news.

So, yes, life can sometimes be hard, but it's not meant to harm us, but to bring us to an expected end- an ending of us being in purpose and fruitfulness. Yes, we all have our lot in life and we all are different, but whatever the difference is, it's meant to be used for the glory of God; not to be bitter, fearful, angry (for long), in despair, doubt or confusion. However, it's to take ALL the experiences we have and will encounter, and as the senior folks would say, "chew the meat" (those things I can and what is good for me) and "spit out the bones" (those things that I cannot use and that are harmful for me) and count it all good.

God did not call us to wallow in self-pity, regret or shame. Remember to forget how and when things happened but choose to remember, what it produced. Remember to forget the who but choose to remember, what you have become. It doesn't make any sense to reminisce on what could have been if, it leads you to a place of depression, regrets and ungrateful. Quick question here, what are you adding to your life going down that road of memory lane?

Forget it and relieve yourself of bondage that ties you to the things of the past that will keep you from pressing forward. Out of the mouth of my dear Aunt Bert, who is living her best life in her 90s "It is what it is!"

DONT MOVE

He only is my rock and my salvation; he is my defense; I shall not be moved.

Psalm 62:6

This world pandemic has caused humanity to be moved in so many levels. It has moved us to fear. It has moved us to hysteria. It has moved us to rebellion. It has moved us to forgive. It has moved us to love. It has moved us to service. It has moved us to be resourceful. It has moved us to help. It has moved us to seclusion. It has moved us to soul search. It has moved us to de-clutter. It has moved us to share. It has moved us closer. It has moved us to worry. It has moved us to trust. It has moved us not to trust. It has moved us to anger. It has moved us to peace. It has moved us to believe. It has moved us to refrain from believing. It has moved us to pray. It has moved us to do nothing.

It has moved us!

We have been moved!

So how do we "not move" inside a situation that will entice us "to move"?

I'm so glad you asked. Jesus knew that the information, the situation, the experience that Peter was going to encounter with His death was going to shake him to the core. In order for him not to be shaken by it, He prayed that the foundation of his belief, which is FAITH, would not be shaken. In the NLT of Luke 22:32, it says "But I have pleaded in prayer for you, Simon (Peter) that your faith should not fail. So, when you have repented and turned to me again, strengthen your brother."

Jesus knows where we are in life and in this pandemic and He says to us today; Do not be moved or shaken. Do not allow your faith, trust, belief in Me in this season move you to wavering faith; move you to irrational thinking and behaviors that lead you to fear or decisions outside the will of God. Faith is not faith until it's tested.

God is still God. He is God before covid, during covid and after covid. He is God before the storm, during the storm and after the storm. He is God before the marriage, during the marriage and after the divorce. He is God in singleness and widowhood. He is God before you had money, when you had money and after the bankruptcy. He is God before the job, in the job and when the job is no more. He is God before the fight, in the middle of the fight and after you come through the fight.

Come on here!!

Can I encourage you to be strong, in the Lord!

Can I speak life, **YOU** will live in this and through this and **YOU,** will not die!

Can I tell you, don't get weary because there is a promise of reaping if you don't faint!

Can I prophesy, the peace of God that passes all

understanding will keep you in this hour!

Can I tell you, God's report over your life is strength!

Just don't be moved!

BREAK-THROUGH

There hath no temptation taken you but such as is common to man; but God is faithful who will not suffer you to tempted above that you are able; but will with the temptation also make away to escape.

1 Corinthians 10:13

Right out the gate, you don't have to be hindered, stopped or blocked. You don't have to be out of the game or feel like you can't or won't recover. This is a news flash for someone today. You can and will Break- Through to the other side.

The children of Israel thought they couldn't escape Egypt. Joseph thought he was going to be in the pit for a lifetime. Jonah thought he was stuck in the fish forever. David thought he would never come out of the cave. Sampson thought he missed the mark. Hannah thought she would always be barren. (Are you finding yourself in here, somewhere?) Elijah thought he was the only one in the fight. Jehosophat thought they were going to be defeated. Lot thought he was going to be destroyed. The woman in adultery just knew she was going to be stoned. Nahum thought he couldn't be healed. Esther thought she and her people were going to be annihilated.....UNTIL...

In the lives of these people, they learned to break

through the opposition, the obstacles and the mountains that were set before them. Even though it looked like it was a "dead situation", something good prevailed when the people decided not to give up and move forward. It was scary, Yes. It was unexpected, Yes. It was unfair, Yes. BUT, not impossible. There was light at the end of the tunnel. There was green pasture on the other side. You won't know the outcome, the favor, the blessing until you break-through.

Don't allow fear, doubt or worry to keep you immobilized. There is always a blessing with your name on it. You just have to break-through and get it!

THE "BE" ATTITUDES

By: Lashay Joi Townsand

BE CONFIDENT

For the Lord will be your confidence and will keep your foot from being caught.

Proverbs 3:26

Confidence is the best thing a woman can wear. There are days where you feel great and there are other days where you feel insecure. That's life. But you should know that God makes no mistake, even when he made you. Everything has a purpose, from the birds in the air to God's most complex creation, humans. You have a calling; you have a God ordained mission. How cool is that? God chose YOU to carry out his word in a way only you could do. Don't be anxious; be proud of yourself and who you do it for. You are made in the greatest image. Be confident in it! After all, you got this. Now rock in your calling.

BE BOLD

Delight yourself in the Lord. And He will give you the desire of your heart.

Psalm 37:4

Being bold isn't about drawing negative attention. It is about being confident with who you are and what you believe in. This makes you unique.

Being bold is using your God given voice to speak His gospel. This may be scary, but don't worry about what others will say. Stay focused on your MISSION. You have to be brave enough to listen to your heart. God doesn't bless us with discernment for nothing. Be strong enough to live the life you have always dreamt of. So live life to the fullest in Christ and enjoy the blessing!

BE BEAUTIFUL

You are altogether beautiful, my darling, and there is no blemish in you.

Song of Solomon 4:7

In the Song of Solomon, this is exactly what God thinks when he looks at you! Your beauty inside and out should match. True beauty is within and makes the outer appearance even more stunning.

Showcase your beauty in all that you do; whether it be helping a senior citizen cross the street, feeding the homeless, encouraging someone who is discouraged, or even praying for a stranger in the coffee shop. Let God's beauty shine through you onto others. It creates an amazing domino effect.

BE YOU

If any man is in Christ, he is a new creation...

2 Corinthians 5:17a

God made everyone in their own special way. You are different and made to be set apart and that's awesome! Even twins have a unique traits. Nobody is better at being you than you. Because of Psalm 139:14 we know we are fearfully and wonderfully made. There is nothing to be ashamed of. Whether it's your bright hair colors, wacky sense of style, corny humor or a very interesting tone of voice....IT MAKES YOU UNIQUE. It fits you and only you. God loves us all and He feels so good when He looks at what a great person He made.

WISDOM SPEAKS

Does not wisdom call out? Does not understanding raise her voice?

Proverbs 8:1

An area of struggle, if truth be told, in living the God kind of life or life period is walking in wisdom. See, wisdom calls you to get understanding, not to act prematurely or impulsively, but with sober judgement and patience. Wisdom calls for you not to lean to your own understanding, but to have a reliance and dependency upon God or on others who may have sound advice. Wisdom calls for you to be sober minded and self-controlled. Wisdom requires all the things that we don't want to give but must sacrifice in order to be productive.

In my life, lack of wisdom caused me to make impulsive decisions in regards to relationships, finances, investments just to name a few. And now 10 or 20 years later, I'm coming out, by the grace of God. Sometimes I think if only I had just listened or waited, I wouldn't have had to…..(you can fill in your own blank). What I have learned is that after the experience, I, all of a sudden have great understanding…(lol) and wisdom for the "next" that comes my way.

See, wisdom is a sacrifice of your will and your way. Many times, we don't want the understanding or hear that it's NOT the right timing or the right season or the right person in your life or the right job or the right direction or the right move or the right investment, etc. We want what we want, when we want it, which oftentimes, is now. And many times, it's things or opportunities ordained for us, but we just have to wait a bit. So, can I ask a question? Has not waiting ever cost you, big time?

Let wisdom speak. Get the understanding. Get the information. Get the direction that will impact and set you up for what has been ordained for your life and wait, for there is a due season.

JESUS IS M.I.A.

God is our refuge and strength, always ready to help in times of trouble.

Psalm 46:1 (NLT)

Jesus as Mediator: We deserve death as a result of sin and the enemy wants us to join him in the end because of sin, but Jesus mediates the decision for life or death because of the blood that was shed on calvary. He serves as the middle-man, the peace maker that works between two sides to bring about a settlement. 1 Timothy 2:5 says, "For there is one God and one mediator between God and men, the man Christ Jesus , who gave himself as a ransom for all men..."

Jesus as Intercessor: He prays on our behalf, that God, the Father would intervene in our lives and in our affairs. He brings our matters before the Father for Him to do something about because, we can't. Jesus prayed on behalf of Peter that the matter challenging his faith would not fail. As sitting at the right hand of the Father, He makes intercession for us and when we don't know what to pray, "come on", the Holy Ghost, steps in and prays for us.

Jesus as Advocate: He is our helper, public support, champion who argues our cause in order for us to advance the Kingdom, to be a light in darkness, to be an example that brings God glory. 1 John 2: 1-2 says, "...I write this to you so that you will not sin. But if anyone does sin, we have one who speaks to the Father in our defense-Jesus Christ, the Righteous One. He is the atoning sacrifice for our sins, and not only for ours but also for the sins of the whole world."

Jesus is our M. I. A. that when we go m.i.a. (missing in action), He will come and get us. He will come and help us. He will come and pray for us. He will come and rescue us. He will come and go before us.

PRAY THROUGH IT

Do not be anxious about anything, but through prayer and supplication, with thanksgiving, present your request to God.

Philippians 4:6

    A recent Facebook post from Minister Terrell Wheat said "Prayer tells Heaven I Need Help. Prayer tells hell I have help." Can I add to this awesome quote, that we cannot make it without prayer; without talking to God, our Father and the only way to make it in life, is by praying through it.

    Prayer gets us through the tough times. It's not in a drink; it's not in a drug; it's not pleasing your flesh or self-medication, but it's being able to talk to God about anything and everything. There is no fanfare, glamour or magic remedy or pill. You just have to pull up your britches and pray yourself through it. You just have to talk your way through it. You just have to declare the Word through it. You just have to allow God's council through it. You just have to wrestle through it. You just have to submit through it and at the end, be still.

    I grew up in the era of out of tune pianos, slapping tambourines, hand clapping, foot stomping, moaning mothers and praying deacons, laying on the alter that got a prayer through. That was my foundation. Nobody wants to tarry or wrestle in prayer anymore because we don't think it takes all that. We've become progressive and intellectual with prayer. I know there are all types of prayer that Jesus teaches us, but every now and again, something has to resonate that it's prayer and prayer alone that will get us through it all....

So no matter how anointed we are, no matter how many degrees we may have, no matter how much we think we have or not have, no matter what we endure or not, it is only through prayer that we all will get through these tough times, tough trials, tough situations in order to come out through the other side.

NO LIMITS

Now to him who is able to do immeasurably more than all we ask or imagine, according to his power that is at work within us.

Ephesians 3:20

That which God gives us and calls us to do, He equips us to do. I'm going to say that again. ALL THAT GOD GIVES AND CALLS US TO DO, HE EQUIPS US TO DO! We are the ones that limit God and limit ourselves. We are the ones that think God can't because what we see and hear is insurmountable. We believe that we can't because of what we see and hear within us is not attainable.

I wholeheartedly believe that if God said I can do it, I'm going to try and I'm going to do it. If He said it's going to happen for me, I believe that it will, and I shift to that place of belief. I get tripped up when people around me don't believe or speak negatively about what I'm believing God for in prayer. I know the fact of the matter before me, however, there is a truth (the Word or promise about the situation) about the matter that I choose to believe. I hate to keep silent, but sometimes I have to (Wisdom Speaks) in order to get the break-through, the answer, the position that I'm believing God for. I have to shut out the noise (dissenting opinions). I remember on two occasions where I allowed the opinions of others to limit my momentum in ministry and what I believe God was continuing to call me to. Even though I do understand that God may shift seasons, I just wonder if the decisions made was God or "man" limiting me. We were traveling extensively to California to host Women United in the Faith Conferences. One year, which ended being the last year, was faced with lack of registration and one of our organizers for that area lost her voice. There were so many voices (opinions) in my ear, even though I was of the mind set we push and travel anyway. I felt as though I was standing alone. I didn't want the team that was traveling from different places to come to an empty conference, but I believed God. Even if it were a remnant, we would worship and preach as if it were a hundred. However, my belief, didn't convince me to pursue, so we canceled. I often wonder to this day, what if we had pressed our way…there's no telling what God would have done.

The other occasion was for one of our local conferences that we held in December. December conferences can always be tricky due to the weather, but we had always braved through it and everything would be fine. This particular year, we experienced a very bad snowstorm. Even though the people pressed their way and the crowd was lower than usual, I was very discouraged and felt defeated. So, the next year, we decided not to host the conferences for fear of the weather. How silly, but I did it. As a result of that one decision, another ministry took the date that we usually had, therefore, making it a competing pathway for the ministry conferences in the future. Again, I wondered, what if my feelings hadn't gotten in the way of this decision…

So, don't be afraid of what's on your life to do and accomplish. Don't second guess yourself in what you need to be doing. Don't doubt God in what He can and will do on your behalf.

I CAN SEE CLEARLY NOW

And Elisha prayed, O Lord, open his eyes so he may see.

2 Kings 6:17

As we face this pandemic of Covid 19, we are seeing (and hearing) a lot of things: increased death rates, dismal reports of states in trouble, protest and the unrest in people, defiance and disobedience against state ordinances, people in fear, contradictions in government, frustration in families as parents are now co-teachers, loss of jobs, high unemployment rates, and the list could go on and on. If we aren't careful, we will begin to believe that we have entered into the end; that we will never recover. Even before Covid, some of you were seeing your life dismally and in despair thinking and wanting the end to come, but God said not so.

In the text of 2 Kings 6:15, the servant became alarmed, because he saw horses and chariots of strong force that had surrounded the city and he had no idea what was going to happen and what they should do. In the state of affairs that we find ourselves in globally and personally, all we may see is what is strong and forceful in our face. Some of us may be like the widow woman that wants to take her last and die, but God is still saying not so. Open up your eyes to see that "those that are with us are more than those that are against us." God opened the servant's eyes to see the hills full of horses and chariots of fire all around Elisha (them). Can I prophesy, the fire is around you. The fire surrounding you is God's protection, His covering, His purity that nothing will harm you.

Can you see that in the midst of the pandemic: God is raising up people from their bed of affliction, the gospel is being preached and proclaimed like never before through social media, people are being a blessing to one another, Nations are seeking God and praying, the body of Christ is being revived, businesses and giftings are being birthed, purposes are being restored, God is giving us time (I'm finishing this project), God is providing; families are being healed and coming together. God is saving. People are praying like never-before. God is sending revival and igniting the hearts for good (even though there may be evil). Can you see good things coming out of this instead of what's in the news?

Instead of looking down and seeing what's wrong, let's look up and see the goodness of the Lord still in the land of the living.

BE FAITHFUL

And will not God bring about justice for his chosen ones, who cry out to him day and night...he will see that they get justice, and quickly. However, when the Son of Man comes, will he find on the earth.

Luke 18:8

We always testify to the faithfulness of God, but the real question is, are we faithful to the God of our salvation. According to Luke 18:8b clause, "when the Son of Man comes, will he find faith on the earth?"

It's easy to quit when life gets hard; when situations get hard. It's easy to walk away and not have the patience to endure. It's easy to check out and throw in the towel and not fight for what is rightfully yours. We don't want to go through the issues in life sometimes, because we have options; options in attitude that we don't have to deal with this, therefore we don't. I marvel and not that I always agree in some instances with marriages of old. Women just stuck it out regardless of husband actions, children action or extra demands of service. They prayed, forgave, believed and fought for the sanctity of marriage and family because of God. That principle and the Word of God (the believing husband or wife sanctifies the unbelieving spouse) helped me in fighting for a marriage and family that the enemy wanted to destroy because there was destiny assigned to us together!!

We don't want to suffer, but suffering is inevitable in the believer's life. Our Lord and Savior suffered, therefore, there are things in our life that will cause us to suffer. But in the suffering which is for a "little while" will He find his children faithful. Can we be faithful not to cave under pressure? Can we be faithful to serve when everyone else quits? Can we be faithful to stand and believe when no one else agrees? Can we be faithful in integrity when people tell you to compromise? Can we be faithful to give when the well (appears) to be dry? Can we be faithful to what is "true" when others say we're being foolish?

I encourage us in the Word, 1 Peter 3:13-17 says, Who is going to harm you if you're eager to do good? But even if you should suffer for what is right, you are blessed. Do not fear what they fear; do not be frightened. But in your hearts set aside Christ as Lord. Always be prepared to give an answer to everyone who asks you to give an answer the reason for the hope that you have. But do this with gentleness and respect, keeping a clear conscience, so that those who speak maliciously against your good behaviors in Christ may be ashamed of their slander. It is better if it is God's will to suffer for doing good than for doing evil.

So be faithful to stand with and for a God who is faithful to us.

BE STILL AND KNOW

Be still and know that I am God: I will be exalted among the nations, I will be exalted among the earth.

Psalm 46:10

I consider myself to be an high achiever, a go getter, an influencer in the things that God has called for me to accomplish. With the help of the Lord, I'm excited in achieving the greater works that he has spoken of. However, there are times that the "mover and shaker" in me gets ahead of God. In my zeal, I sometimes missed the timing of God because I didn't wait for all the information pertaining to the assignment. Waiting and waiting some more were vital lessons that I had to learn.

Can I be real? Sometimes, I don't like waiting because I see things are getting out of control or I feel there's something else that can be done, or I wonder how long God. And when I ask God if there's anything that I've missed or is there anything else I can do, there is silence on the other side. Those moments serve as reminders that God has everything that concerns me. It's in His hands, always has been and will be. So, my response, then and always is to be still. Be still Meta. Quiet your spirit and trust in God who is able to do all things, but fail. Trust in God who is faithful. Trust in God who never lost a battle. Trust in God who will keep what I commit to Him. Trust in God whose Word will accomplish what I send it out to do. Trust in God and don't lean to what I think or feel.

The Serenity Prayer comes to mind that I will paraphrase for this context: There are some things I can change, and I do, but those things I can't, I relinquish them to you. And I keep my eyes on you.

So, I encourage you and remind you, especially us mothers or us parents, we cannot change things about our children, that for some, is weighing so heavy on your hearts. We cannot live in regret. We give them (and any situations) to Jesus because he's the only one that can change their hearts, mind, spirit and soul. Just Be Still and see the salvation of the Lord. Be Still, intentionally and with self-control to wait. Be Still and know that he is God.

FRESH OIL, FRESH FIRE

Prophetic Utterance:

I prophesy to your now, that God is stirring you, that God is touching you, that God is restoring you, that God is recalibrating your future. God is setting you ablaze for such a time as this. That any devastation, disappointments, frustrations will turn for good and used for His glory.

Even as God is closing some doors in your life that was meant for evil, He is turning things around, that your joy is returning, your hope is being refueled, your strength is being renewed. The enemy thought he had you, but God called you out and made a way of escape.

I declare that God is for you, He is more than the world that is against you. He will not suffer you to be moved. But He gives you grace to endure the race. He gives you stamina to stand. He endows you with power and might. And his anointing will break every yoke. We declare your mind is free, for whom the son has set free is free indeed. You are called to live in purpose and on purpose because of the Godhead presence of the Lord in your life. You will live and not die.

You are victorious. You are more than a conqueror. You have come this far by faith, leaning on Him, trusting in Him, depending on Him. There are rivers of living waters flowing through you now. I declare you will not thirst again, because you are filled with His Spirit. The Spirit of the Living God breath on you now, fall fresh on you now. Get up now and knock the dust off your shoes, off your soul, run the race that is before you. Just as the prophet Elijah ran before Ahab, I speak that you run the race that is set before you with vigor.

So I declare that there is a fresh oil to invigorate you and a fresh fire to stir you in Jesus Name!

GROWTH MINDSET

Do not conform any longer to the pattern of this world, but, be transformed by the renewing of your mind. Then you will be able to test and approve what God's will is-his good, pleasing and perfect will.

Romans 12:2

A term that we use to describe and discuss student progress is having a "growth mindset." We believe that we can increase student's abilities and performance by helping them to learn more effectively. What we are looking for is the growth of student progress in relation to the instruction being delivered. An educational goal for children, of course, is to see them grow.

Another aspect for growth mindset is not only for the growth of students, but for the teaching staff that is in service to them. Look, over these 40 years in education, children have changed, education has changed, delivery models have changed, curriculum has changed and if we're not careful in changing along with it, we will become (and some of us already have) extinct. The "cheese" has moved, and unless we move with it, we will be frustrated in and with the process.

From this scripture, we are admonished in the Lord, to change our thinking; to think differently, to get a different perspective, get a different perception when it comes to our life and our living. There is a purpose and plan for who we are and what we are to be, that cannot be fulfilled unless our minds change about who we are and what we are to do and become. When we realize that we are a new person when the spirit of God comes into our lives, we need a growth mindset to recalibrate our thoughts that we may know who we are in Christ. We cannot live this new life now with an old mentality. It is only when we allow Him to grow us up; when we desire to want to change that our minds are transformed. Transformed means to make a dramatic change in form, appearance or character. If we are to know what is pleasing to God in this hour that we may live, our minds have to dramatically be changed to his likeness. It is through this change in thinking that we can be free.

Our prayer to God: God give us (me) the mind of Christ. Let the mind of Christ be in us (me) that I may live.

RESET

**Revive us, and we will call on your name.
Restore us, O Lord God Almighty; and make your
face shine upon us, that we may be saved.**

Psalm 80: 18b, 19

Sometimes when I use my GPS to get from one destination to another, I may choose to take a different route than what I'm being told. It is at those moments then, that I choose to ignore the guidance of the route planner because I already know the way and will get to my destination. There are other times, however, that I miss the guidance provided or think I know where I am going, only to be rerouted in order for me to get back on track, that I may reach my destination.

When we have God's GPS (The Holy Spirit & The Word of God) in our lives, and we choose to take a different path, because we think we know the way or we may be in fear or we don't want to obey or we are selfish or prideful or we are used to what we know, we get rerouted in order for us to get to our destination. If truth be told, we will obey God's GPS or either we won't.

Jonah had an assignment that he didn't want to obey because of his pride, his biases towards others and his thoughts about the matter of God's Word for Ninevah.

As a result, he chose to take another path, only to be rerouted by the Lord by way of a great fish. In reading this story again, I wonder, if Jonah's obedience to being reset was only because we wanted out of the fish. Because after he obeyed the assignment, he was still an angry person (that's another message, in itself) about God's compassion and grace on a repented nation.

My encouragement for us is that God knows the plans He has for us and sometimes we get off the road, we make the pit stops, we make the detours knowingly and unknowingly. The good news is that He reroutes us; He resets us; He revives us; He gives us another chance (And God knows I appreciate every chance that He gives me). He is going to get the glory out of our lives.

I pray that you not lean to your understanding, but to acknowledge Him, that he may reset and redirect your life.

ENCOURAGE YOURSELF AGAIN

Rejoice in the Lord always, I will say it again. Rejoice!

Philippians 4:4

"Re" is a prefix that means again. There are times and probably all the time that we have to do things again. Rejoicing and having encouragement are one of those things. No matter how often we get knocked down, disappointment, hurt or whatever gets "our goat", we have to learn to shake it off and smile again, rejoice again, be happy again, be encouraged again.

Life around us can knock us for a loop, but we have to learn to take a licking and keep on ticking. We have to learn to shake the dust off our shoes and keep it moving. We have to learn to live and not die. We have to keep stride when there are temporary setbacks. How can this be done? I'm so glad you asked me again…

Put on the garment of praise for the spirit of heaviness (Isaiah 61:3)

Sing and praise (Paul & Silas)

Continue to dream (Joseph)

Experience the faithfulness of God (Noah, during the

flood)

    Become (John became a writer on the Isle of Patmos)

    Obedience (widow who fed Elijah)

    Worship (woman with the alabaster jar)

    Seek Him (Hannah)

    Fellowship (disciples were in the upper room)

    Pray (Luke 18:1)

    Live in purpose and on purpose (cloud of witnesses in Hebrews 12)

ENCOURAGE YOURSELF:

WORDS OF LIFE & HOPE

In this 30 day journey, what words of encouragement have you been speaking or declaring to yourself and/or situation?

Date:_____

_____
_____
_____
_____
_____
_____
_____
_____
_____
_____
_____
_____
_____
_____
_____
_____

Date:_____

Date:_____

Date:_____

Date:_____

Date:_____

Date:_____

Date:_____

Date:_____

Date:_____

Date:_____

Date:_____

Date:_____

Date:_____

Date:_____

Date:_____

Date:_____

Date:

Date:_____

Date:_____

Date:_____

Date:_____

Date:_____

Date:_____

Date:_____

Date:_____

Date:_____

Date:_____

Date:_____

Date:_____

Date:_____

ABOUT THE AUTHOR

Meta J. Townsand, a native of Washington, D.C., currently resides in Grand Rapids, Michigan. She and her husband, Elder Larry, are the founders of New Creation Ministries, Inc. since 1995 in addition to faithful service in local assemblies.

A woman of prayer, lover of the Word, she enjoys sharing and teaching the Word enthusiastically in various platforms. Her inspiring messages for life are not only for the body of Christ, but for those that are lost and feel hopeless. She has served as Christian Education Director, Sunday School and Bible School teacher, devotional writer, community ministry planner, adjunct professor at Grace Bible College. She has earned a MAT degree from Calvin University and has served in public education for over 40 years.

New Creation Ministries sponsors several events: Educators Prayer Call on Mondays, Intercessors Prayer Call on Fridays and quarterly Intercessors Arise Prayer Gathering, spiritual and educational mentoring. Her favorite scripture is 2 Corinthians 5:17, If any man is in Christ, he is a new

creation. Old things have passed away and behold, all things become new.

Contact Information:

Email: metaj58@gmail.com

Edert1950@gmail.com

Newcreationministries@comcast.net

www.ingramcontent.com/pod-product-compliance
Lightning Source LLC
Chambersburg PA
CBHW071124090426
42736CB00012B/2008